A WORM'S HOME

BY ANNIE TEMPLE

HOUGHTON MIFFLIN   BOSTON

Hello.

I'm an earthworm. I'd like to welcome you to my home.

I live in a wonderful place with plenty of food, fresh air, and just the right amount of moisture.

I live in the soil.

When some people come into my home, all they see is dirt. Soil is a lot more than dirt. Soil includes ground up and partly dissolved rocks and minerals.

Soil contains water and air too. This is a good thing for me. I need water to keep my skin moist. I get air from the soil. Can you believe it? I breathe through my skin!

Soil also has humus in it. Humus is small bits of dead plants and animals. Humus is usually brown or black, so it can change the color of the soil. Humus is food for me. It is what I eat.

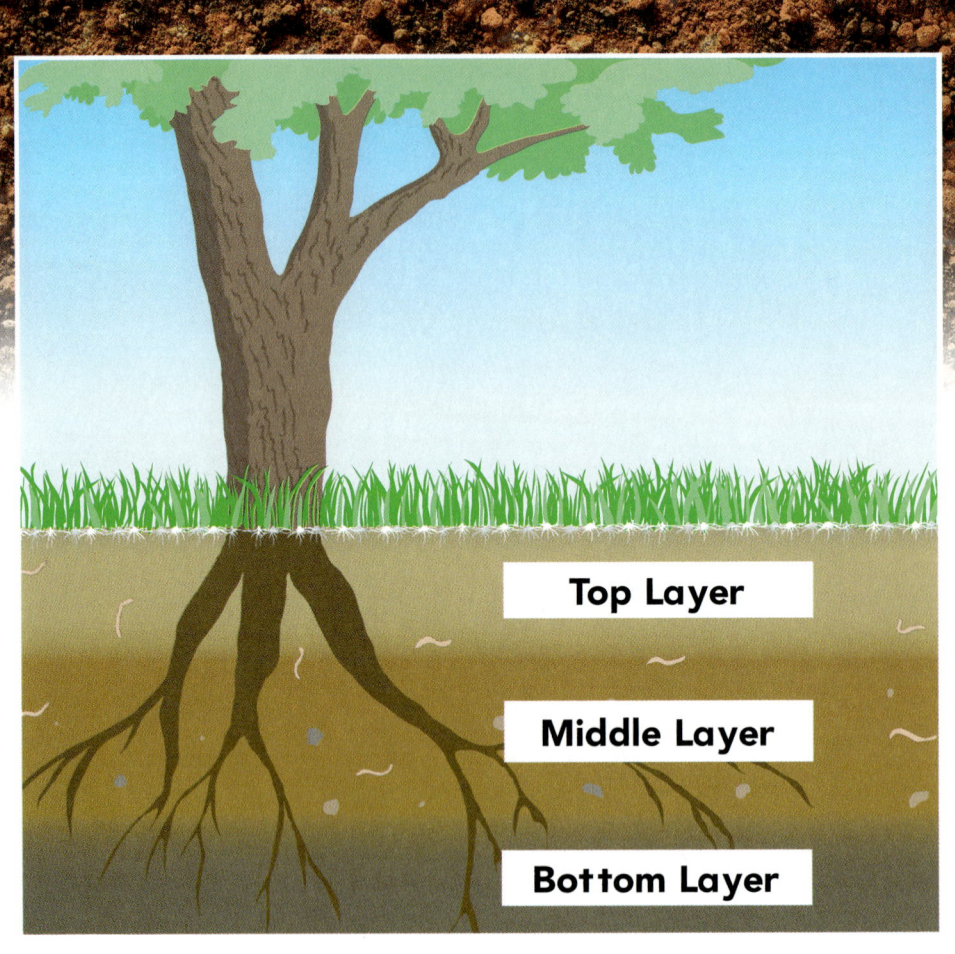

My home has different layers. The top layer is full of humus, lots of roots, and plenty of air and water. The middle layer has small rocks and some humus. The bottom layer is made up of tree roots and bedrock. Earthworms mostly live in the top two layers where there is food, air, and water.

I do a lot to fix up my home. When I eat humus, I grind it into even smaller bits. This way, plants can use it as food. But I do more than that.

When I crawl through soil, I mix the layers. My tunnels help bring air, water, and food to other living things. Even the slime on my skin is good for the soil.

Next time you see an earthworm like me, think about how I care for the soil, my home.